SIGHT WORD FLUENCY READING

FIVE Languages

Improve Your Child's Reading Skills

English German French Spanish - Polish

Kuh

vache

cow

vaca

krowa

The cow is standing up.

Sonne

soleil

sun

dom

słońce

The sun is very bright.

Auto

voiture

car

coche

samochód

My car is fast

Haus   maison

house

casa   dom

We live in the same house.

Katze   chat

cat

gato   kot

That cat is adorable.

Wind   vent

wind

viento   wiatr

The wind blows the leaves.

Geld   argent

money

dinero   pieniądze

I save money in my piggy bank.

Schuh   chaussure

shoe

zapato   but

I have new shoes.

Papier   papier

paper

papel   papier

I like to color on paper.

Uhr   l'horloge

watch

reloj   zegar

My watch is ticking.

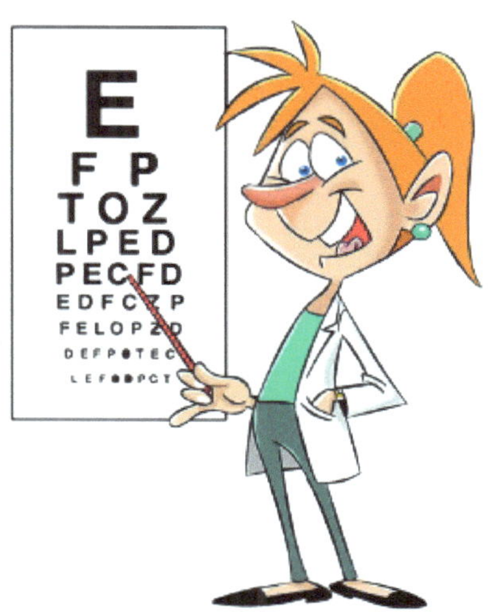

Diagramm   graphique

chart

gráfico   wykres

What does your medical chart say?

Nest   nid

nest

nido   gniazdo

The bird has a nest.

Tür

porte

door

puerta

drzwi

He is knocking on the door.

Junge

garçon

boy

chico

chłopiec

The boy is eating dinner.

Blume

fleur

flower

flor

kwiat

She is holding a flower.

Zeit   temps

time

hora   czas

He is telling the time.

Mantel   manteau

coat

saco   płaszcz

She is wearing her coat.

---

griechisch   grec

Greek

griego   grecki

Have you ever had Greek food?

Spiel

jeu

game

juegos

Gry

What game is it?

Auge

œil

eye

ojo

oko

He is closing his eyes.

Puppe

poupée

doll

muñeca

lalka

She is hugging her doll.

face

Gesicht

visage

cara

Twarz

They were at the face painting booth.

rabbit

Hase

lapin

conejo

Królik

The rabbit wants to play.

school

Schule

école

colegio

szkoła

They are going to school.

Hügel   colline

hill

colina   wzgórze

The house is on the hill.

Frankreich   france

France

francia   Francja

Have you ever been to France?

Familie   famille

family

familia   rodzina

How big is your family?

Unternehmen
compagnie

company

empresa
firma

What company do you work for?

Kopf
tête

head

cabeza
głowa

She has a hat on her head.

Schwester
sœur

sister

hermana
siostra

She is my sister.

Geburtstag anniversaire

birthday

cumpleaños urodziny

Today is my birthday.

Ding chose

thing

cosa rzecz

I am thinking of many things.

Füße pieds

feet

pies stopy

His feet are swollen.

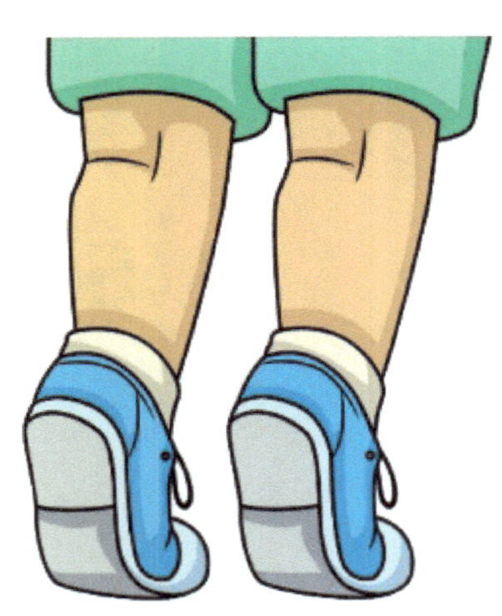

Ring   bague

ring

anillo   pierścień

The bird is holding a ring.

Apfel   pomme

apple

manzana   jabłko

Apples are a popular fruit.

Idee   idée

idea

idea   pomysł

I have an idea!

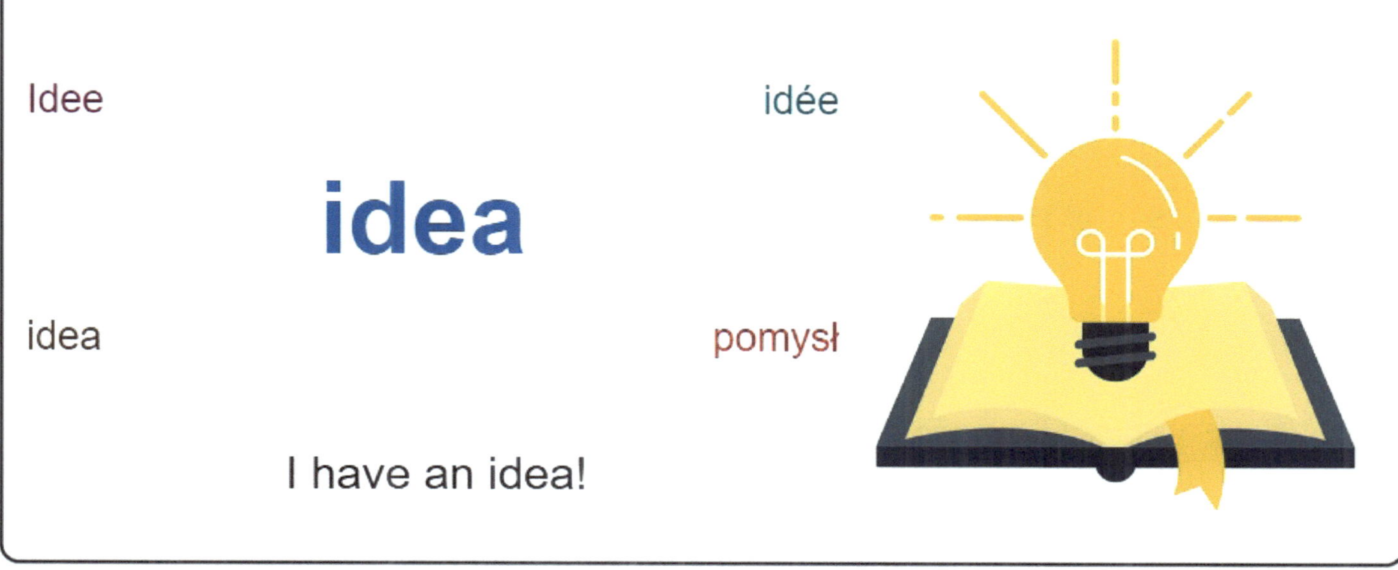

Tabelle

table

table

mesa

stół

There is a toy on the table.

Fußboden

sol

floor

suelo

piętro

The girl sits on the floor.

Seil

corde

rope

cuerda

lina

Do you have any rope?

Büro — bureau

office

oficina — gabinet

Do you need any office supplies?

Nase — nez

nose

nariz — nos

My nose is running.

Bauernhof — ferme

farm

granja — wylądować

The farm has lots of animals.

Wasser

l'eau

water

agua

woda

He is drinking water.

Hacke

houe

hoe

azada

motyka

Use a hoe in the garden.

Samen

la graine

seed

semilla

nasionko

We will plant the seeds.

Brot   pain

bread

un pan   chleb

She is baking some bread.

Baby   bébé

baby

bebé   dziecko

The baby is crawling.

Säule   colonne

column

columna   kolumna

Did you read the newspaper column?

Farmer
fermier
farmer
agricultor
rolnik
The farmer had a farm.

frisch
frais
fresh
fresco
świeży
All the fruit is fresh.

Alphabet
alphabet
letter
alfabeto
alfabet
Learn English letters is fun.

Mann

homme

man

hombre

mężczyzna

This man is my dad.

Bett

lit

bed

cama

łóżko

We all share three beds.

Garten

jardin

garden

jardín

ogród

They are going to the garden.

oben | haut

top

tapas | Top

We like to play with tops.

Name | nom

name

nombre | imię

My name is Joe.

Schnee | neige

snow

nieve | śnieg

I have fun in the snow.

Bein   jambe

leg

pierna   noga

My leg is feeling better.

Holz   bois

wood

madera   drewno

He plays with wooden blocks

Fenster   fenêtre

window

ventana   okno

The window is open.

bird

The bird is dancing happily.

four

There were four of them.

pig

She is lying on the pig.

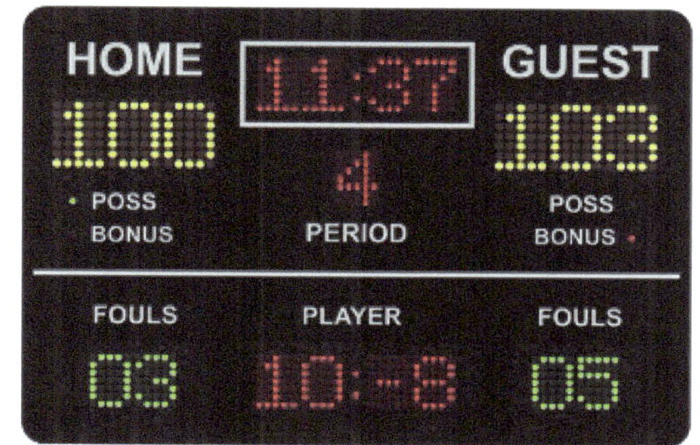

What was the final score?

What is the symbol for oxygen?

He is taking some pictures.

Gras — herbe

grass

césped — trawa

The goat is eating the grass.

Auf Wiedersehen — au revoir

goodbye

adiós — do widzenia

The bear is saying goodbye.

Vater — père

father

papá — tata

He is a nice father.

Männer

hommes

men

hombres

mężczyźni

The men are arguing.

Baumwolle

coton

cotton

algodón

bawełna

A q-tip is made of cotton.

Kinder

les enfants

children

niños

dzieci

Four children sang.

Ort	endroit
place	
sitio	miejsce

place

This is my favorite place.

Tag	journée
day	
día	dzień

day

This day is the 30th.

Ente	canard
duck	
pato	kaczka

duck

The duck is swimming.

Pferd   cheval

horse

caballo   koń

The horse is galloping.

Mädchen   fille

girl

niña   dziewczyna

The girl is pretty.

Regen   pluie

rain

lluvia   deszcz

We love the rain!

Sitz   siège

seat

asiento   siedzenie

The girls took a seat in the sand.

Kirche   église

church

iglesia   kościół

Did you go to church?

Seite   page

page

página   strona

Please turn the page.

Zuhause

maison

home

casa

Dom

He drew a picture of his home.

Essen

aliments

food

comida

jedzenie

They made a lot of food.

Milch

lait

milk

leche

mleko

The baby is drinking milk.

Rose   rose

rose

rosa   Róża

Thank you for the rose.

Eichhörnchen   écureuil

squirrel

ardilla   wiewiórka

The squirrel is on the tree.

Bruder   frère

brother

hermano   brat

They are brothers.

Boden   sol

ground

suelo   ziemia

It plays a trick on the ground.

Ei   oeuf

egg

huevo   jajko

The bunny has many eggs.

Spielzeug   jouet

toy

juguete   zabawka

He has a whole box of toys.

Nacht nuit

night

noche noc

We sleep at night.

Hähnchen poulet

chicken

pollo kurczak

The chicken is laying eggs.

Baum arbre

tree

árbol drzewo

She is sitting under a tree.

Boot	bateau
boat	
barco	łódź

The boat is sailing.

Stühle	chaises
chair	
sillas	krzesła

He is sitting on the chair.

Feuer	feu
fire	
fuego	ogień

Fire is hot.

Beispiel exemple

example

ejemplo przykład

This is an example of a bird.

Kitty minou

kitty

gatito koteczek

I like my kitty.

Gewehr pistolet

gun

pistola pistolety

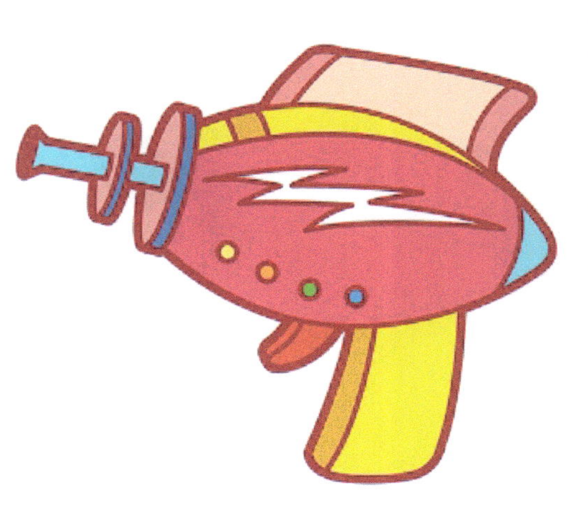

We played with a water gun.

Schaf — mouton

sheep

oveja — owca

The sheep have fluffy wool.

Kinder — les enfants

children

niños — dzieci

The children are playing.

Party — fête

party

fiesta — przyjęcie

I love to go to parties.

Morgen   matin

morning

mañana   ranek

I wake up in the morning.

Straße   rue

street

calle   ulica

They walk across the street.

Kuchen   gâteau

cake

pastel   ciasto

The cake is white and pink.

Hand	main

hand

mano	dłoń

You should wash your hands.

Stock	bâton

stick

palo	kij

He is playing sticks.

Robin	robin

robin

robin	rudzik

The robin is helping Santa.

Stadt
ville

city

ciudad
Miasto

He worked in the city.

Hund
chien

dog

perro
pies

The dog wants to eat sweets.

Weg
façon

way

camino
droga

They find a way back home.

Box   boîte

box

caja   pudełko

The box is full of clothes.

Ball   balle

ball

pelota   piłka

He is bouncing the ball.

Bedingungen   conditions

conditions

condiciones   warunki

What are the weather conditions.

Lied   chanson

song

canciones   piosenki

She is singing a song.

Mutter   mère

mother

madre   mama

My mother loves me.

Glocke   cloche

bell

campana   dzwon

I hear the bell ringing!

Bär   ours

bear

oso   Niedźwiedź

The bear likes to eat honey.

Fisch   poisson

fish

pez   ryba

There are two fish.

Mais   blé

corn

maíz   kukurydza

I grow corn in the garden.